Summer School

Leadership Lessons
from the Lady Titans

By Gary Brown

This book is dedicated to Rochelle Brown.
The best wife a man could ever have.

Rochelle, thanks for helping Meredith and Bethany become the individuals they are and for saying yes when I asked you to marry me. The three of you are the greatest blessings a man could receive in this life.

Thanks also to the families who gave up nights and weekends to make the Lady Titans possible. Your friendship will always be important to our family and it would be hard to imagine life without each one of you. You have made a genuine difference in our lives.

The Lady Titan Family

Landy Birch
Parents: Jim & Becky
Sisters: Whitney & Calli

Meredith Brown
Parents: Gary & Rochelle
Sister: Bethany

Adrienne Cain
Parents: Martin & Theresa
Brother: Travis

Starr Harmon
Parents: Pam & Walker
Brother: Chris

Lauren Jackson
Parents: Hugh & Lori
Sister: Abby Jackson

Jessica Mays
Parents: Tim & Dena
Brothers: Colten & Spencer

Shatara Stone
Mother: Linda Chapman
Sister: Brittany Stone-Carter

Table of Contents

I am learning all the time. The tombstone will be my diploma.
Eartha Kitt

A single conversation with a wise man is
better than ten years of study.
Chinese Proverb

You learn something every day if you pay attention.
Ray LeBlond

I don't think much of a man who is not
wiser today than he was yesterday.
Abraham Lincoln

All the world is a laboratory to the inquiring mind.
Martin H. Fischer

I am defeated, and know it, if I meet any human being
from whom I find myself unable to learn anything.
George Herbert Palmer

Whoever loves instruction loves knowledge,
but he who hates correction is stupid.
Proverbs 12:1

Introduction

It was working in the first half. The Lady Titans were making passes from the perimeter to inside players that either made a strong move to the goal or quickly kicked it back outside to girls that had pretty good touch from behind the three-point line.

At the half, these Arkansas girls from a very small school led a much bigger Kansas team by five points. They also looked very confident while shooting and talking during the five minute halftime break.

If the first half was all thumbs up, the second half was just the opposite. Like any good opponent, the Kansas City team started to use their significantly taller girls to their advantage and took the lead from the Lady Titans.

After a couple of minutes, momentum shifted back to the Lady Titans as they took the lead back, but were not able to push it beyond three to five points.

With a little over five minutes left, they faced another stiff run from the Kansas City team, and with just over two minutes left, the Titans found their lead was gone.

In summer basketball, where the clock runs continuously, two minutes is not much time, and we had been in this position way too many times before.

The pattern was predictable. Play well. Make a few mistakes. Melt down. Lose the game. Would it be different today? Would three summers of work finally pay off and the young women of the Lady Titans finally grasp what we had worked on and talked about so many times?

When the timeout was called I was not sure what new strategy we would employ. Was it time to be firm and call them out, or to try and inspire them? Walker, my fellow coach, knew just what to do. He walked into the huddle of dejected looks and asked them, with a big smile on his face, a question: "What would you want to eat right now?"

The girls looked at him as if he had lost his mind, but then Meredith said she wanted a steak. Starr thought that sounded good. Shatara wanted potato soup. They each shared their ideal treat at that moment, with Walker sharing his desired indulgence last. He just smiled and said, "A cool piece of key lime pie would sure be good right now."

We broke the huddle and you could sense a change as the girls walked back on the court with laughter in their voice and calm in their souls.

Shatara's quickness started us off when she stepped in front of a pass and streaked down the court. She was picked up at the top of the key by a pesky defender, and what would have normally been a drive to the goal or rushed shot became a quick outlet pass to a hustling Meredith on the wing, who buried the three to tie the game up.

When we were back on defense they tried to drive our baseline, but Adrienne stepped down to quickly block access to the goal and Lauren tipped a pass that was heading inside. Starr grabbed the ball and started down the court when she spotted Shatara and ripped a pass to her that resulted in a layup

Back on defense again, Starr created a turnover and made a pass to Shatara, who got the ball to Meredith with a pass that resulted in another two points, and you knew that with just a minute to play a win was at hand.

They seized the momentum back in a firm, solid way, and you could see the life drain from our opposition. You also could see our team had learned the secrets to successful basketball: teamwork, hustle, practice and perseverance. When the buzzer sounded the girls hugged each other with joy and beamed the smile of the victorious.

An hour or so later the girls and their families met at Gates Barbecue for one last meal together before we loaded up and started the five-hour drive home.

The room we were eating in was empty except for our traveling party. We had been doing this for what was now the completion of three summers together. The girls were all going into tenth grade, except for one girl who was just a grade behind them, and we knew this trip might just be the last one for this particular group of girls, their brothers, sisters and parents. We had grown close over these years. We enjoyed good times together and bad times. We lost way more games than we won. We had grown into a very close group that knew each other's faults while also knowing the good that was inside every person in the room.

We especially knew the good possessed by these young ladies. I sat alone during most of the meal in a back booth from which every face could be seen and every voice heard. Over the course of the meal something became very obvious to me.

For three summers these girls had listened to sermons on the value of team and hard work. They listened patiently to every lecture about perseverance and how they could never back down from challenges in life. They endured time-outs where they were called out and ones where they were cheered.

After all the time we had spent together here is the realization that came to me as we were sitting there: through all of our experiences together, the greatest lessons were not what we left them with, but perhaps what they had taught us in these years.

In the pages that follow you will learn what can be taught by a gritty and determined group of young women. You will also learn lessons our ball girl and the families of this little gang provided along the way.

If you have the courage to take them to heart and practice them in your life, you will become like the Lady Titans. You will be a winner. Good luck, and may you have the same unyielding spirit they have collectively and individually.

Trust only movement. Life happens at the level
of events, not of words. Trust movement.
Alfred Adler

Few things help an individual more than to place responsibility
upon him, and to let him know that you trust him.
Booker T. Washington

Trust no one unless you have eaten much salt with him.
Cicero

You may be deceived if you trust too much, but you
will live in torment if you don't trust enough.
Frank Crane

Trust in the Lord with all your heart, and lean
not on your own understanding; in all your ways
acknowledge Him, and He shall direct your paths.
Proverbs 3:5–6

Lesson One: Trust Matters

One of our players ran to the scorer's table to check into the game, and as she took her place on the floor the girl she was replacing came trotting over to the bench.

As they swapped places in the playing rotation it never dawned on me to question why or even give it a second thought. The person who made the decision was trusted. It was not until after the game that it occurred to me how really significant a decision it was, and in particular my unquestioning acceptance of it.

This was very different from what happened a few years prior, when working with someone else, as decisions over playing time and almost everything else would become way too often.

There is one occasion in particular that reveals all a person needs to know about the working relationship we had.

We were losing by twenty to twenty-five points with only minutes left in the game when I beckoned someone to go into the game. Our obvious differences in the goals we had for the team were highlighted when he made a remark about how putting her in would kill any chance we had of winning. At this point it became necessary for me to point out how things could not get much worse than they were, and playing other people would give us needed experience for the school year. A few more words were exchanged under our breath and he finally stormed off the bench in front of the girls and their families.

We were swimming in the opposite direction over the team's objectives, and the miles between us were increasing quickly the entire time. There were other arguments about practice commitments, offenses and how to discipline the team that kept reinforcing the differences.

We argued even when we were working off the same page. One game I grabbed a sub to go in for another player just as his daughter made a mistake. He assumed his daughter was being replaced and gave me an earful about pulling players right after a mistake. He never considered the sub was going in for someone else. We also made a real point not to pull a player just after a mistake to keep from hurting her confidence.

What was the problem? I did not trust him, and, in reality, he did not trust me.

With Walker the situation was just the opposite. Every year we were together it was always evident everyone associated with the team was going the same direction and pulling for each other. He made substitutions because we trusted each other and the decisions each made.

Trust is a very special commodity. Our extension of it and the timing of when we release it to someone else is one of the more complex decisions we make in life.

We meet people and make some determination of how far into our world we will let them go, always holding back our trust until time and experience allow us to let them completely in.

Meanwhile, we desire to be complimented in one of the highest possible forms: being considered trustworthy.

Giving trust to others is significant because it exposes you, and obviously others become vulnerable when they extend it. The giving of it is a significant action because sometimes your decision will have been a right one and other times you will wince at how blind you were to give your trust away.

In the office there are times when you have to be able to talk to someone about what you are seeing and thinking about particular strategies and opportunities for your company and maybe your career.

You pick someone to confide in and develop a relationship with. Over the course of time you give greater extensions of trust and think you have found something unique: a trusting relationship.

If time proves your decision to be a good one, the collaboration between the two of you can produce fantastic, exciting and impactful work. Congratulations.

What happens when your judgment turns out to be off base? Besides the hurt you feel at being betrayed, there can also be a severe impact to hitting the targets you set, and, even worse, you can find your career being derailed by someone who used your trust to create an advantage for himself or herself.

In personal relationships, missing the call on who should and should not get your trust can be even more devastating to your well-being and others you care greatly for.

Choose to confide in a person who does not regard your confidences with care and see how much damage can be left in the wake.

Marriage represents the highest form of relationship where trust resides. When it is broken, it can be incredibly difficult to regain. When trust is kept between a husband and wife, it becomes the gateway to a fulfilling and complete life.

The lesson is simple. When picking a person with whom to enter any worthwhile venture, make sure you can trust him or her while allowing time, experience and actions to dictate how high a level of trust can be given.

It was through all three of these items that Walker Harmon proved he was a person who could be trusted in handling both the big, and little things, with our team.

Trust is one of the cornerstones required to build a team of any type. As a foundational block it connects players and coaches so everyone can be counted on to do what is right as you work to achieve something bigger than what any individual is seeking. It gives credibility to the idea that people are making decisions that are best for everyone and not self-centered ones. Trust allows people to freely express themselves, creates celebration when one member of a team experiences success and keeps jealousy at bay.

It is trust that allows Walker to speak honestly when he does not like something within our team.

If confession is good for the soul, then here it goes. There were times when I rode officials pretty hard. Well, maybe not pretty hard; maybe more like really, really hard.

From the tip-off until the final whistle, every call was something I saw differently and better. We were an incredible team because from my vantage point, we committed no fouls, and if we turned the ball over it was only because the other team had.

After one game when we were walking to the parking lot Walker pulled me over and asked for a minute to talk. He told me I really needed to tone it down. First, he told me my actions were becoming a distraction to the team. Second, yelling at an idiot did not make him call the game any better and third, it really made me look kind of foolish as well.

That hurt. Mostly because every word he said was true. My behavior changed (most of the time) because of his honesty, and we became a better team as a result.

If he had not demonstrated the courage to speak honestly with me, it would have hurt our team. He knew that saying what needed to be said was more important than saying what I wanted to hear.

It is a special form of trust that allows someone to give you honest counsel instead of lip service or saying what they think you want to hear.

As a leader it will be your obligation to make sure you enable people to have this ability. If you respond negatively to their thoughts that don't align with yours, then they will learn to keep them inside, which only deprives you of what you need to hear to keep the team moving forward.

Some people have been burned so often when they have expressed their thoughts that it will require your best effort at times to seek them out and convince them to share their ideas. With consistent effort it will eventually become a part of the culture around you and help produce results that will matter to you and the people working with you.

If you are in a role where you need to be honest with someone, it will be helpful to keep a few pointers in mind.

First, pick a right moment to speak. If Walker had spoken his mind right after the game, he might have found the reception poorer with all of the emotions of a game still boiling. Instead he waited until the girls were out of earshot and we had watched a few minutes of another game.

He also pointed out how my actions were impacting everyone who was part of the team and hindering our ability to be successful. In all of this, there was one really important trick he pulled off. He smiled the whole time and made sure I knew he was not angry with me. When he told me what an idiot I could be perceived as, he even let out a little laugh at the notion that I would want that to happen. It was really direct, really kind and really effective.

The things Walker did to prove he was someone to be trusted are the same things you need to look for in people as you let them into your circle. They are also the traits you will need to demonstrate so others will feel you are trustworthy. Here are a few of them for your consideration:

Do what you say you'll do, when you say you'll do it. If there is one single item to keep in mind to gain the trust of others, this would be it.

People are really good at making promises, and many times even better at not keeping them.

When you say you are going to do something, you need to get it done on time in the way that was expected, if it is within your power at all. If you are not going to deliver as you said, you need to make sure those who are counting on you know why you failed and how you will make it right. You will fail at some point. How you respond will speak volumes about you to others.

Being trustworthy means caring about more than yourself. People who give you a trust believe you have consideration for them. Be worthy of that emotion. Hear what they are telling you and give thought to how the situation is impacting them. React in a way that shows you have given real consideration to what they need.

It may require taking baby steps to convince someone else that you really are thinking of his or her interests, but over time, by proving to be a worthy ally, you will be trusted with even greater items and more responsibility.

You will have to be vulnerable. Trust is about emotion. It is about being open and honest. To gain it or give it, you open yourself up to the possibility of being let down or hurt. Given that life would be very lonely if we never trusted others, it is essential that we make ourselves vulnerable.

It will happen. You will give trust to someone and he or she will let you down. It will be painful and make you angry. You will experience a wide range of emotions.

When this happens, you should learn from the experience, but to make life as great as it can be, you have to move beyond these feelings and be open to someone all over again. Doing this is a lot tougher than writing it, but it can be done.

What I learned from Walker Harmon? A trusted advisor who will give you honest counsel is a great asset. It can be the difference in success and failure.

✿

You can't hit a home run unless you step up to the plate.
You can't catch fish unless you put your line in the
water. You can't reach your goals if you don't try.
Unknown

The vision must be followed by the venture. It is not enough
to stare up the steps—we must step up the stairs.
Vance Havner

It is a most mortifying reflection for a man to consider what
he has done, compared to what he might have done.
Samuel Johnson

Only those who will risk going too far can
possibly find out how far one can go.
T. S. Eliot

Between the great things we cannot do and the small things
we will not do, the danger is that we shall do nothing.
Adolph Monod

Let your eyes look straight ahead, and your eyelids
look right before you. Ponder the path of your feet,
and let all your ways be established. Do not turn to
the right or the left; remove your foot from evil.
Proverbs 4:25–27

Lesson Two: Time to Step It Up

Our leading scorer and key ball handler, Shatara, sprained her ankle. It was just a few minutes later when Adrienne, our leading rebounder, went down with one as well. It was our Tuesday practice and we had a tournament that weekend.

Friday morning, just a few hours before our departure for the weekend, the phone rang and it was one of the girls talking about her plans for the weekend changing and saying she would not be able to make the trip.

We only had seven players, and after losing the two with sprained ankles, we invited one of the former Lady Titans to play with us for a weekend to give us a sub. We were now back down to five players. It would be hard to go without a bench.

After much discussion we decided to put a uniform on our water girl and let her go in if there was a real need in a close game. All of the other girls were in high school. She had just finished the fourth grade.

We woke up on Saturday morning and Meredith, one of our guards, was sick. She thought she might be able to make a go of it, but after giving it a real effort, her stomach ultimately won after just one half of play.

This left us with one guard to handle the point, a forward who did not like to shoot or dribble who would have to be her primary back court help, one post player, a last-minute recruit and a fourth grader.

In spite of all this, it may have been the best single weekend the Lady Titans ever had, and we did not even win a game. It was our weekend once, and as the saying goes, "it was the best of times and it was the worst of times."

Starr is very quiet when you first meet her, but once she becomes comfortable around you, her dry sense of humor emerges and you get a sense of just how smart and wise she is. We have never had a team captain, but if the girls were to select one, my guess is that Starr would be their choice. She is consistent in character and very confident about who she is.

In sports Starr has displayed talent in a number of areas and is not afraid to try new things. She is probably one of the few track and field participants that does both the pole vault and discus. She is a sprinter, but when called upon gladly participates in distance races. Wherever the team needs her, she goes.

That is her nature. It is also her personality to let other people stand in the spotlight while she does her thing in the background. She would rather make a pass to an open teammate than take a shot, and she is an excellent shooter.

She is the ultimate team player, but that weekend would have to be different. Starr was going to have to not only score points for us she was going to have to play the point position. After all, she was the only true guard we had left that was not in the fourth grade.

Landy, one year behind the other Lady Titans in school, did not like to shoot. She wanted to rebound and play defense. She also did not like to dribble the ball.

Like Starr, she played volleyball and was an almost dominant player, but in basketball she just spent most of her school season riding the bench. We wanted her to be a Lady Titan again because of the ability she had shown in the past and to help her rediscover her passion for playing. Landy was the only player we could realistically expect to help Starr with ball-handling duties under any true pressure.

Lauren was an inside player who relied more on finesse and quickness to get into position for rebounds. She had a fast release and soft touch when shooting that made her automatic from the free-throw line, but during games she did not get enough touches to score as she was capable of doing. That weekend she would also have to get some points, but more importantly she would have to be a more physical player with Adrienne out of the lineup for the weekend with her bad ankle.

As the weekend of games progressed, we played teams with Division I basketball prospects on them. Our little ragtag group managed to hold their own throughout most of the games, only allowing the final margins to get out of hand when their legs didn't have any "go" left in them. So, what was it that made that weekend so special for everyone associated with the Lady Titans? When those young people were challenged to step up, that is exactly what they did. All three did what they were asked to do.

It started with Lauren pushing and shoving back at a bigger and stronger player who she normally would have played more softly against if we'd had our normal lineup.

Lauren is a wonderful young lady who truly would not only never hurt a fly but, if she knew she had, would take it home and nurture it back to health. In one game the year before, she had accidentally become tangled up with a player from another team who fell pretty hard, one of those moments that happen in basketball.

No whistle blew and we were sprinting the other way in a hurry. In the midst of all this action, Lauren stopped, helped the girl up and apologized to her. This is just her nature. It will serve her well in life, but we had been telling her for years to become more aggressive on the floor…that it was all right. That weekend, she stepped it up.

Early in one game a more physical girl from the other team was pushing Lauren away from the lane pretty aggressively to keep her from getting position. There was some pinching and elbowing that is typical of rough play in the paint.

At some point early on, enough was enough for Lauren. She used her own elbow to get her position back, and picked up a foul. The other girl had a lip that was a little bloody, but the rest of the day she respected Lauren working for position and stopped with her cheap shots. It was just a few minutes later when the official stopped the game and warned Lauren about rough play. I don't think I had ever been so proud of a player for getting in trouble.

Lauren smiled a little about it after the game. She also grabbed a bunch of big rebounds that weekend and played like a lion on defense. It carried over the rest of the summer for our team and made us better.

Who knew? We had not seen it at practice ever and never in a game before, but when she had to handle the ball under pressure, Landy looked great.

She made bold decisions and did not hesitate to get down the floor with the ball in hand. When the other team trapped our other players in the backcourt, Landy would get in position to catch the ball and make them pay for ignoring her.

On the other end of the floor she would look for the open seam and drive to the goal or take a shot. Some went in, many missed, but at least she was shooting the ball and trying to be part of the offense.

When Starr could not get to the top of the key to handle the point because of defensive pressure, Landy did not hesitate to step up and lead the offense, but most important Landy learned her role was to find ways to contribute beyond what she had been accepting of.

Starr was the real highlight of the weekend. She went from passive role player to leader with a purpose in just five games. She played almost flawlessly at the point when faced with pressure, having only a handful of turnovers.

She ran the offense like a veteran and made sure adjustments from the bench were implemented. She moved the ball around the perimeter like never before and was not reluctant to take shots when she needed to. In one game she knocked down three straight three-pointers, lifting us from being behind into the lead.

Her finest moment was yet to come, though. At the end of one game, it was up to her to make something happen if we were going to win, and the way she handled the situation spoke volumes about how she stepped up that weekend.

With only four or five seconds left, we were down three and inbounding the ball under the far goal. There was a play we had practiced for a moment just like this, and now it was time to execute it. Problem was, the person we wanted to take the shot was back at the hotel sick, the first alternate was on the bench with a bad ankle and Starr had always practiced another role for this particular situation.

When the ball was thrown in to start play it was way off target, but Landy made a great catch and without missing a beat turned and got the ball to Starr, who calmly turned and released an arching shot that was on line and high enough... but bounced just off the front of the rim.

She did something she had never expected to do, while under pressure, in the spotlight, without practice and missed it by less than a quarter of an inch. Watching the game that day, an uninformed spectator may have thought she missed the mark. From the perspective of those who knew how much of a leader and player she became that weekend, her shot was dead on.

Among the many lessons from that weekend: people will step up when you call on them to, but if you never create an expectation for them to, then it won't happen very often.

From that weekend on, Starr became a different basketball player, and it made her teams better. She was willing to take charge. She was willing to handle the ball. She was willing to launch her graceful shot with more confidence than before. She remains somewhat quiet, but she knows how to lead. She no longer defers to others when it is time to break a press, but will get the ball down the floor. She is also bolder in putting up a shot or driving to the goal.

It happened this particular weekend and continues today because it became expected of her. Starr, Lauren and Landy all have a natural humility at their core. On that weekend when they had to, though, they discovered a good dose of courage and faith to "step it up." It was even more exciting to see them keep stepping up when everyone was healthy again.

Are you stepping up? When you look at your career do you see someone who is bold when it comes to his or her work or someone that just tries to compliment those around him or her while staying out of the spotlight?

At home, are you letting a full life pass you by and just accepting the routine as the way it is?

In any situation you encounter, are you just trying to get through, or are you making it count?

If it is time for you to step up and you are unsure of how to do it, try some of these ideas and see what kind of results you get.

Look for a small problem that needs ownership. In every company there are issues that are small in scope, but need to be taken care of. Be the person who tells the boss you want to take care of a particular challenge.

It can be as simple as making sure the refrigerator is cleaned out once a week or managing the birthday calendar. It may be as complex as creating a system for communicating information that is falling through the cracks currently.

However small, however big it might be, finding something you can step up to and call your own says you are a person who is not afraid to take something square on. After claiming ownership, though, do the unexpected. Exceed everyone's expectations in your approach to the opportunity.

Make "value creation" a part of your job description. Most of us get comfortable with the results we get, and once we are settled in we develop habits that reinforce that comfort level.

From now on, spend a set amount time each week considering ways you can help reduce costs or increase revenue. At times you will identify changes that only produce small results, while other times you may come across bigger winners.

Here is the point: if you are showing your boss ideas that create value for the company, then you will be rewarded at some point. Even if your ideas are not implemented or credited to you, you will develop a reputation as someone who is thinking.

In addition you will find increased confidence as your mind keeps looking for the next "value creation" opportunity. Never tire of thinking in different ways as you pursue value creation. From a first idea, a second one is born, and then a third. One of them might just turn out to be the right one. The more ideas you create, the greater the possibilities.

Connect the dots. One of the most difficult tasks in a company is creating ways to streamline processes. Look at the responsibilities your group at work has. Who are you serving upstream and downstream? Once you understand who is going to use your work, consider how you can make their function more efficient.

Look at what people are sending you that is not necessary and does not need to be done. If you can develop the ability to see and understand a process from the starting point all the way through the final user, then you have a unique ability to help others accomplish their responsibilities up and down the chain while also creating efficiencies benefitting those who will be the ultimate users of the service or product being offered.

When all the dots are not connected to each other it is inevitable that something is going through the cracks. When you tighten this up, you are making a genuine difference.

Stop deferring to the eager beavers. When you want to get something done, give it to someone who is already busy.

That expression has been around for a long time, and there are enough people who are really eager to prove themselves or have such a reputation for getting things done that people just naturally defer to them. Stop being one of the people who thinks someone else is more qualified or will do a better job than you.

In order to successfully step up you are going to have to be willing to stick your neck out from time to time and take a chance. If you take no chances, you will have very limited opportunities for successes.

Being willing to grab hold of opportunities that come up is a critical key to stepping up.

Be ready to fail. Whenever you step up you are taking a chance on not being successful. The odds in many cases are that you will fail. Accept that and get over it.

There is not a person who has experienced success in any meaningful way who did not also fail in measurable ways as well. When you fail, you gain experience that can be invaluable the next time you have a chance to step up.

Think of Starr taking that last-second shot. She missed it, but the next time she will know what it feels like to have the ball in her hands with that kind of pressure and to come really, really close to great success.

If I have the chance to coach her again, I will make sure she gets to take that shot. She has been there and I believe she will get it done.

If she had not been called on to step it up that one weekend, who would have ever known she had it in her?

It's important to know that words don't move mountains.
Work, exacting work, moves mountains.
Danilo Dolci

I know the price of success: dedication, hard work, and an
unremitting devotion to the things you want to see happen.
Frank Lloyd Wright

I don't wait for moods. You accomplish nothing if you do that.
Your mind must know it has got to get down to work.
Pearl S. Buck

Don't waste life in doubts and fears; spend yourself
on the work before you, well assured that the right
performance of this hour's duties will be the best
preparation for the hours and ages that will follow it.
Ralph Waldo Emerson

Go to the ant, thou sluggard; consider her ways, and be wise.
Proverbs 6:6

Lesson Three: Getting Better Means Working Hard

Summer basketball becomes tedious at some point for almost every player. After all, summer is a time for swimming pools, hanging out with friends, and just being lazy. The heat and slower pace that comes with it seem to win everyone over eventually. Almost everyone.

Our summer routine was pretty consistent. Each week we would have a full practice. The girls had to make a set number of shots three times during the week, and one night a week we opened the gym up for anyone that might want a little individual help or extra work.

Early each summer there was usually pretty good attendance at the optional practices, but the numbers would ebb and flow as the weeks went by. One night when it was really hot and we were coming off a weekend tournament, none of the girls were waiting for me when I arrived at the gym about five minutes before practice time.

As the clock ticked closer to the time when they knew the gym would be available, hope was growing inside me that maybe they all were going to blow off the night, which would allow me time to go home and just hang out with my family.

Then she pulled into the parking lot with her mom at the wheel. Adrienne bounced out of the car with her big smile and a "Hello, Mr. Brown." She then spent the next hour and a half practicing her turnaround shot from the free-throw line and her moves from the low post.

Early on I just sat and watched from the sideline, but after a bit she wanted me to come play defense against her. She practiced her moves while being pushed on and missed way more than she made. When it was time to close the gym up, she kept begging for just a few more minutes of practice time, like she was a little kid who was just told it was time to get out of the pool.

Adrienne worked hard like this on a daily basis. If the gym was not open, she was at home making Travis, her older brother, rebound by the outdoor lights illuminating their driveway. At every practice she would push herself and only play at an all-out speed. She did not seem to even know another gear or how to get through practice by pacing herself like so many other players at all levels do.

When the final whistle would blow, she would be spent and ready for a shower, but before going she would practice shooting until her mom or dad would insist it was time to go. Her intensity would make you tired just watching how hard she went after it.

Adrienne worked very hard but so far was not enjoying the results she wanted. She played very little in games. There was nothing graceful about her moves, and she made way more mistakes than she should have.

But over time, you could see little improvements in her game and bigger growth in her confidence.

A summer of hard work paid off for her in our last tournament in Colorado, when Adrienne received the ball behind the three-point line twice in a row and did not hesitate to let the ball fly. The first time she shot the ball, we winced a little on the bench. That was not a shot she was supposed to take. Then it went in, barely moving the net. The next time down, she banged another long three in.

Adrienne was starting to arrive as a basketball player.

It would have been easy to dismiss her work ethic as being driven by a desire to gain more playing time, but even after she earned a starting position, her intensity for improvement never diminished. She may have even worked harder to become a better player.

At practice she would listen intently to instruction. During drills she did not go through the motions, but really worked to be better. In competitive situations at practice, she wanted to win. In games she took it as a personal insult if the other team beat her for a rebound.

Adrienne pushed herself to get better whenever she stepped on the floor. She also kept making Travis rebound for her at home. In her junior year of basketball Adrienne was one of two girls from our school named All-Conference. Do you think her hard work had anything to do with this?

Jessica had a lot of the same attitude. We played a tournament one weekend where she struggled on offense. She was not comfortable with the ball in the paint and committed several turnovers. Even catching the ball was a struggle. She was clearly frustrated with her play and was really down leaving the court.

When we talked later, she told me she wanted to score more. I have never met a player who did not express this sentiment at some point. I told her that points would come, but playing defense, passing and getting rebounds were all critical to a team's success as well and not to discount her contributions in these areas. It was obvious from her expression that she was not very comforted.

We played again two weekends later. Jessica was a different offensive player. She would receive the pass in the high post and turn with confidence to face the goal. If she had a shot, she would take it. If the shot was not there, she would make a crisp pass to an open player. She even put the ball on the floor at times and went to the goal with it. This sudden surge of offensive energy even paid off in her defensive activity level and intensity going after rebounds.

Watching her smile after each game and eavesdropping on her conversations with her dad after games I learned what had happened. She had spent the last two weeks putting in overtime to improve not just her moves, but catching the ball and making the turn to the goal. She did this at home on her own, and with the help of her little brothers. She wanted to get better.

Like Adrienne, she kept working until she was meeting her expectations. Then once she reached those, she set the bar even higher.

It is not fashionable to say this anymore, but good things come to people who embrace hard work as a lifestyle.

In our society, where every kid receives honors on awards day and trophies are handed out just because you show up, hard work is seen as unnecessary. While it may not be fashionable to say it, it is true. What expectations do you have in life? To be rewarded just for showing up? If your plan does not include hard work, then don't whine when you don't reach your goal.

Remember how Jessica talked about wanting to score more points in a game? That has been a comment made by more than one player. Anyone who has coached or played at any level has heard someone say those magic words. Odds are they have heard many people say it. What have they not seen? They have not been witnesses to many kids that will get out day after day after grueling day and make one hundred, two hundred, or more shots. They have not had the opportunity to watch a kid stand endlessly at a free-throw line until he or she makes 90 percent or better of his or her free throws.

This type of practice is dull, time consuming, and, more than anything else, very lonely. In basketball, this is what it takes to become better. It is also hard work that drives success in almost every other pursuit in life. It is not fashionable to say it, but it is the truth.

How is the passion created inside a person to work hard? Why do some people "get it" while others don't?

If you look at people who are successful, they share common traits that drive their hard work. Establishing these in your life can help you rise above the ordinary and become more of what you want to be.

Know where you want to wind up. It seems the happiest people in life have a magnificent obsession. Most important, they are able to create a visual in their mind of what life will be like when they reach their prize. They can see the road they have to travel to get where they want to be from where they are. When bumps occur they remain undeterred in their pursuit, because they know their destination is worth the price they have to pay, and they know it can be reached.

Can you see where you want to go?

Planning the process. Once you know where you want to go and start moving forward, you need to make sure your activities will lead you to the destination you are seeking.

Becoming a better shooter in basketball is not very complex. You have to shoot the ball and shoot it often. One approach is to just step on the court and randomly shoot until you are satisfied with the day's work. To become a really good shooter, though, you probably need a more thought-out plan. Making a certain number of shots from specific spots will help you develop muscle memory and confidence that will allow you to knock down shots in the clutch. In addition you will want to catch and shoot the ball under conditions as close as possible to those you will find in a game.

The first level of planning was better than no plan, but the second one is more likely to help you reach your goal. Good planning will lead to better outcomes than random activities.

Don't leave a third undone. My good friend Larry Armstrong is constantly saying, "There are doers and there are chewers." Larry is a doer. His career as a chemist was not bringing him the satisfaction he wanted in life personally or financially, so he went back to school and became a neurosurgeon.

If you know what you want your life to look like and have created a plan to get there, you have only done two thirds of what it takes.

You still have to get busy.

You have a plan, but now it is time to actually do something. Every day you need to do something to help you get closer to your goal. Every day you don't is one day further away from getting home. If you don't do something with your plan, you will be doing something...just not what your heart desires.

Do something besides just sitting there. Dreams are fantastic. They look pretty, and when they involve our view of life as we want it to be, they are often nearly perfect.

It is easy to allow these dreams to remain fantasies that look nice and are never accomplished. Years pass by and the dream evolves, but it never moves from the realm of what might be into what is possible because no action is taken to bring it to life.

People who have a magnificent obsession and can see the road ahead get up and do something. If you never get off the couch and get busy taking the steps necessary to make your dream live, then guess what? It won't happen.

Getting where you want to go will require forward progress from your actions. It won't come from lying on the couch thinking how nice it might be.

Believe in your pursuit. You can see where you are going, you know what it will take to get there, and you are walking the walk. But count on something going wrong, and also depend on people not being able to see what you see.

When these moments occur in your pursuit of a magnificent obsession, will you be able to remain optimistic about the journey you are on?

The world is full of people who will tell you why something can't be done. You have to be a continual voice that says, "It can and will be done." You have to be the true believer in your dream. If you don't believe, you will not work as hard as you can to be where you see yourself standing.

If you have a vision of where you want to wind up, it is only a fantasy until you come up with a plan and act to get there.

Adrienne and Jessica are on their way. How about you?

My goal in sailing isn't to be brilliant or flashy in individual
races, just to be consistent over the long run.
Dennis Conner

Look to make your course regular, that men may
know beforehand what they may expect.
Francis Bacon

A consistent man believes in destiny, a capricious man in chance.
Benjamin Disraeli

Let your character be kept up the very end,
just as it began, and so be consistent.
Horace

The only way a man can remain consistent amid
changing circumstances is to change with them while
preserving the same dominating purpose.
Winston Churchill

Most men will proclaim each his own goodness,
But who can find a faithful man?
Proverbs 20:6

Lesson Four: Value Reliability

Naïve believes success in sports is not defined by winning and losing games. The Lady Titans would not be confused with teams that had tons of success on the court. They were constantly improving as players and, more importantly, as people. These were our objectives as we faced all-star team after all-star team.

There was one team from our area that defined success in the more traditional manner: wins and losses. They did not lose very often over the years they played together as a team, and players' participation was based on how good they were. Their team not only performed well locally, but also on a broader national stage as they traveled the country to play in tournaments where, more times than not, they brought home the winners' hardware.

Their coach was a person I respected. He took young ladies from tough circumstances and made them work hard to improve their lives. We had coached together early on. A few of the Lady Titans had played ball with some of team locally in their early grades and enjoyed visiting with them.

Seeing each other at tournaments led to an easy friendliness over the years. We also respected each other. We respected them because of the talent they had. They respected our girls because they knew we would never stop playing hard, even though the outcome was really determined before the game started.

It was the first game of a new summer, and they were the team we would be playing.

Every game we would set goals for what outcome we wanted and discuss them with the girls. This game the goals were pretty simple. We just wanted to make sure we were solid on how to run a new offense we would be using.

It was during the early minutes of the first half when Starr and Meredith were struggling to line up correctly in their perimeter positions. Since they were both missing their mark, it was probably poor coaching that had them in the wrong spots.

We took an early timeout to draw up their positioning for them and sent the team back on the court. We had the ball and were setting up on offense when Meredith lined up in the wrong spot again. It was then I did something I would not have done to any other player.

My scream, "What are you doing? We just showed you where to go!" could be heard all over the gym and sounded pretty angry. Our next trip down on offense, I was still not very happy when the ball was stolen from us and the fast break was on.

I don't remember who turned the ball over, but I do remember Meredith making a dive at a pass from one of their players to another in transition to cause a loose ball that we retrieved. I also then remember watching her roll over, holding her wrist while fighting back tears.

Meredith does not cry when injured—she has her mother's toughness—but her pain was obvious. In addition to immediate concern over her injury, I also felt like a dog. Just seconds

34

before she busted her gut to make a defensive stop, I let her have it for lining up in the wrong spot. I would not have done that to any other player. This one was my daughter.

As we got Meredith settled on the bench one of our parents, a physician, came over to look at her wrist and encouraged us to get an x-ray. Another came over and the second opinion was the same.

After the game we loaded her up and went to a local hospital where our good friend Larry Armstrong greeted us. He took one look at Meredith's arm and had the same concern as the others about a broken bone.

Medical technology gave us good news that there was not a break, but just a bad sprain. Meredith was done for this weekend, but should be able to go for our next tournament.

We returned to the hotel, where Meredith was consoled by her teammates and irritated by the brace she was supposed to wear. We had one more game to play that night and we showed up to play with only six players since we would not be able to use Meredith.

Before the game she wandered onto the floor to see if she could catch the ball very well. It hurt, but more frustrating to her was the brace she was wearing. Off it came and she resumed catching the ball and gradually found her wrist loosening up.

The ball was tossed into the air for the opening tip and the game quickly became one of those up-and-down-the-floor gassers that leave your tongue hanging out. Our girls were tired and the other team had a much deeper bench.

Meredith knew her friends needed a break, so she asked to go in. We reluctantly agreed and told her not to be very aggressive.

It was useless instruction. She entered the game and played as hard as ever. Her shot was off, but the rest of her game was as consistent as always. She handled the ball some, made really good passes and played tenacious defense. She went after loose balls and went headfirst into piles to tie it up. If she had finished as the second or third leading scorer, it would have been a typical, steady game for her.

Meredith is the type of player that coaches talk about needing all the time yet don't really appreciate when they have them. She understands the team is more important than she is, recognizes what her role is and goes about doing it day after day and game after game.

Her opponents look at her size, but underestimate her big heart. There is a role for her to play and she delivers it. She is not going to make many plays that leave your jaw dropping with wonder at how she did it, but she is also not going to leave you shaking your head very often at a mistake in a critical situation.

She is going to make you really proud watching her dive after every loose ball and challenge every shot within reach. Her legs, hips and arms stay bruised from the start of basketball until two weeks after the season ends.

While teams need stars to carry the load when it comes to scoring, they need even more players who are steady and show up every time they step on the court to contribute in key ways that won't make many highlight reels, but are the subtle difference between winning and losing.

In a world where the phrase "reality television star" is common and fleeting fame is pursued via YouTube and other wired media, it seems everyone desperately wants his or her time in the spotlight.

Given the number of people who want to "be the one," it is still true that some of the biggest contributors to the success of a team or other organization are the quiet ones who show up every single day doing what is asked of them and understand that the bigger picture is more important than any individual issues they may have.

As a person who leads others, it is important that you know who these people are and, even more critical, that you make sure they know how valuable they are to what is being done.

They also need to know how grateful you are for the way they go about their responsibilities. While your stars may make the world turn in many ways, everything would quickly grind to a halt if all of the pluggers stopped showing up.

If you are one of the people doing the right things in the right way every day, you also need to understand your worth to the goals of your organization. Eliminate the unheralded customer service group or distribution team and you'll find out just how good the superstar salesman really is.

Here are some reasons why people who make it happen every day are so critical to a team's success:

They are dependable. This may seem like a statement of the obvious, but think of how few people that are counted on to deliver something on a deadline get it done without having to be reminded constantly or asked where it is after the established window has passed.

When people do not get assignments done on time, they slow everything down, with a resulting impact on everyone in front of and behind them in the process.

Dependability is about more than meeting deadlines. It is also about being there when you are supposed to be *and* when you need to be. In our culture today, people have an ever-expanding list of reasons to miss out on commitments they make. Most of them do not fall into the category of necessary or urgent, but their pursuit of a growing number of commitments detracts from those that are primary or were established earlier.

In order to be where you should be, you have to respect a fast-running clock enough to not do everything you want and instead focus on what matters the most.

When you commit to anything, you should know what the time expectations are and then be willing to meet them in a way that allows you to put your focus where it needs to be, when it is supposed to be there.

When you find yourself constantly arriving late or texting when you are supposed to be doing something else, then you have become less than dependable. You are also telling people who are engaged in the activity at hand that whatever you are doing is way more important than they are.

In my early career years, several friends would gather on a regular basis to talk about life and participate in a ritual I came to call "clocking importance."

People are clocking importance when they want to tell you how many hours they are working and how demanding it is. I played just as much as anyone, but after a few years came to the conclusion that most of the extra hours were the result of time wasted and more could be accomplished in a shorter day if time was used efficiently. I also concluded that the people who were working the longest hours either had employers that did not really care about them or were really disorganized at getting their work done.

Working incredibly long hours is not always what it takes to finish most of what needs to be done, and finish it well.

With that said, it is also important to know that another part of being dependable is knowing there will be times when extra effort will be required of you. This will mean you make personal sacrifices for the good of your pursuit. When people know you are someone who will not only walk the first mile you are asked to, but also the second, they begin to consider your value in a greater light than before.

If showing up is one important factor in establishing a reputation for dependability, then being there when others won't is even better.

They bring lighter bags. When headline performers go on tour, they require in their contracts that certain items will be made available in their dressing rooms and waiting areas.

Demands will be for particular foods, beverages and candies in particular brands, sizes or portions. Many will dictate that a specific type of towel, in specific colors, numbers, and folded in a required manner, be on hand for their use. Others may want a couch made of fabric or leather of a specific type to be obtained for their furniture (which will be used for mere minutes typically) in their dressing area. Some will want all of it. The bigger the star, the greater the ability to demand special treatment.

Pity the cover band that is out performing night after night without all of the fuss, but doing what they do to the best of their ability every time they step on stage.

Entertainment is like most fields. Top talent gets the most attention and the most perks. They can also be the greatest headache you have.

Why does someone have a larger office than *I* do?
My last raise was not big enough.
I'm unhappy with our health care plan.
Our competitors would be glad to get their hands on *me*!

Too many times the emphasis becomes about the individual and not the goals of the larger group. Those who show up and do what is expected of them in the right way every day don't bring this type of baggage with them often. They do what they are supposed to be doing. There is great value in that.

When the stars fall, consistent people shine. It is undeniable that most stars in an organization have talent. They also take big risks that work well sometimes and other times leave an organization gasping for air.

When a star falls, it is usually pretty hard. There are reasons for this that are critical to the success of top performers, but when it happens, it is the smaller lights in the group that are called on to either clean the mess up or get things moving in the right direction again.

A company I worked for experienced significant damage when a tornado of considerable size and strength hit our city. The storm destroyed inventory, offices and raw materials used in our manufacturing. Power was out in much of the area and the ability to readily communicate was challenged as phone lines were down in a large portion of town. Many of our people were also suffering personally with property damage of their own.

The next few days were a dizzying time of "needing to be there" to make decisions and provide leadership. One or two of our most senior people (and stars) were not there. They opted out of the moment because it meant getting into the action and getting their hands dirty in ways that would not provide personal benefit to them.

What was amazing to see, though, was people that stepped forward to make sure there was clarity instead of a void in leadership or decision making. They were people further off the radar than those they stepped in for, but most of them delivered what was needed most critically when chaos was a real possibility. Many of them became the new stars of the company and took it places that were unimaginable before. That is what happens when reliability meets opportunity.

Who are the consistent people around you that get taken for granted? As quickly as you can, make (not find, but make) time to celebrate them and let them know how important they are to what your team is working toward.

If you are one of the steady people and feel unappreciated, take a moment and smile. You are worth way more than you might have realized, even if it is not always recognized.

Want to be a person who can be counted on? It might just be the toughest goal to achieve. Being a star is hard, but being reliable is even tougher.

Are you good enough to be like Meredith?

Walker Harmon in team huddle during a tournament in Branson, Mo.

*Lauren Jackson, Landy Birch and Starr Harmon
paying close attention during a time-out.*

*Shatara Stone signed with Arkansas State out of high
school. She later transferred to Missouri Southern.*

Adrienne Cain facing a slight size disadvantage in Vail, Colorado.

Meredith Brown gets in the air to apply pressure on an inbound pass.

We have always wondered just what Meredith and Starr would be talking about when someone was shooting a free throw.

*Bethany Brown and Caroline Corbin were the
first ball girls for the Lady Titans.*

*Bethany is now taller than Meredith and Starr,
but still looks up to them in many ways.*

Starr and Meredith fired Walker and me as summer coaches for Bethany's team. Meredith and Starr are in the back row, Bethany is second from the left in the middle row.

Dressed up for senior year basketball homecoming at Union Christian Academy. From left to right: Starr Harmon, Shatara Stone, Lauren Jackson, Jessica Mays, Adrienne Cain, Meredith Brown

One last meeting of the Lady Titans before they head off to college. Front row from left: Jessica, Starr, Meredith. Back row from left: Lauren, Shatara, Adrienne

✦

One cannot consent to creep when one feels an impulse to soar.
Helen Keller

If one advances confidently in the direction of his dreams,
and endeavors to live the life which he has imagined, he
will meet with a success unexpected in common hours.
Henry David Thoreau

If you believe in yourself, have dedication and
pride and never quit, you'll be a winner. The price
of victory is high, but so are the rewards.
Paul "Bear" Bryant

Far better it is to dare mighty things, to win glorious triumphs,
even though checkered by failure…than to rank with those
poor spirits who neither enjoy much nor suffer much, because
they live in a grey twilight that knows not victory nor defeat.
Theodore Roosevelt

Don't bother just to be better than your contemporaries
or predecessors. Try to be better than yourself.
William Faulkner

For as he thinks in his heart, so is he.
Proverbs 23:7

Lesson Five: Let Your Stars Shine

Shatara, while not short, was noticeably smaller in stature than the center for the other team, but when the ball came off the backboard from the missed shot, her five-foot-seven-inch frame exploded off the floor and owned the rebound.

Hitting the ground running, she blew by forwards from the other team and made her baseline-to-baseline journey complete by driving strong to the goal, leaving both guards flatfooted as she made a tough move to the basket for two points.

She completed the old-fashioned three-point play by sinking a free throw after a desperation reaching foul was called on one of the defenders. Which game was this in? Pick one.

With Shatara it happens just about every time she plays. When she lines up for the opening tip, it really does not matter who is across from her. If the toss is fair, she will get it more times than not. If you try to belly up on defense against Shatara you will see her back as she sprints to the goal. Give her speed too much respect and she will drain a shot from the perimeter.

Defensively she also has it going on. Let your guard down for a second and she will intercept the pass and be gone. Just when you think you have her beaten in a drive to the goal, watch out, because she will come in from behind and swat the ball out of bounds when you shoot.

For the Lady Titans, she is the one who makes things go on the floor. She can play the game very well, and when she has it going on, it is a beautiful thing to behold.

Shatara is one of those players that drive opposing coaches crazy. They know the burden of ball handling and scoring will rest on her shoulders for the most part, but they still can't shut her down. You can hear them on the sidelines yelling at their players to "stop 33" or "don't let 33 touch the ball." They don't have success very often.

She is a player that coaches love to have in many ways also. She is determined to win and makes the connection between working hard and production.

She has an incredible ability to focus, and she loves it when the game is tight and in her hands.

She loves her teammates as well. There is nothing she would not do for any of them off the court.

On the court, though, there is no denying that she is indeed the star.

Shatara is one of the lucky ones, born with most of the gifts it takes to be a great athlete. Her eye/hand coordination is uncanny. She can see the angles, and her body works in sync with her mind in ways that most people don't enjoy. Her fast-twitch muscles are way above average, and when she wants to make a move, or a second move, it happens in the blink of an eye. She can jump: high or long.

Her track and field accomplishments testify to all of the above. How fast is she? Here are her times at the Arkansas 4A State Track Meet:

100-meter time of 13.38 seconds
200-meter time of 28.03 seconds
400-meter time of 60.78 seconds

The 400-meter time was good enough for a second-place finish, missing the top spot by less than one second.

She also competed in the state's heptathlon, which combines several events into a singular competition between individuals. She finished sixteenth in the event without training for any of the distance events at all.

In between her basketball and track accomplishments, Shatara also found the time to play volleyball and be all-conference. It will be interesting to see how much more she will achieve in her junior and senior years. Those were her accomplishments as just a sophomore.

While she was born with her physical gifts, it is hard to say where the rest of her star power comes from.

Shatara was not born into an easy lifestyle. Many of the girls on our team are from homes with stable and dependable sources of income from parents who have professional practices or careers, while others have parents who operate their own businesses. For Shatara's family of a mother and a sister, life can be more precarious at times.

This might just be what allowed her to maintain such a sharp focus on her relentless pursuit of success. Shatara was driven, from my earliest memories of her, to be better at what she was doing than anyone else.

The girls' first elementary teams were coached by a teacher at school who was not all that much into basketball, so at halftime Shatara would run into the stands and quiz me on what she could be doing better. She was not a starter yet and only played a few minutes in a half, so it was difficult to find much to say, but she wanted to know how to be better.

She would practice constantly. You would never see her without a basketball in her hand then, and today she is the one calling everyone on a snow day to see who wants to head to the gym.

She is passionate in her pursuit to be the best at any game she plays. I remember her losing a game of pop-a-shot that my younger daughter, Bethany, had already mastered and Shatara was seeing for the first time. She kept practicing until she understood the way the game worked perfectly and she felt confident in her ability to take anyone on. Especially Bethany.

She was always working to figure out how to win and how to be better. She was driven in incredible ways. It was all of the above that moved Shatara from the realm of a person with physical gift to being the star of the Lady Titans.

With Shatara you had all the elements that go along with being a star performer, though. If she did not feel her teammates played as well as they should, she let them hear about it. If they failed to get her the ball when she thought they should, they knew it.

There were occasions when she would be surrounded and, instead of passing the ball to an open player, she would force the shot up. She could not understand why others did not perform at her physical level and make plays like she would.

When we lost, she would sulk and pout for hours, and her fellow Lady Titans would walk wide circles around her.

Please understand, we wanted her to take more shots than anyone else. As a team we would not have any chance for success without her physical gifts, and Shatara loved the girls and they all loved her. It was unconditional for all of them. Her star power though, while an absolute must for our team, also kept us from being as good as we could be.

The first problem it created was an attitude among the other girls to just stand around and let Shatara do her thing.

She was so good that they would always defer to her and let her freelance.

This was not Shatara's fault. She would pass the ball to someone else only to have it instantly passed back to her. If they were not going to do anything, she was going to do what she could to make something happen. It was her nature. If the other girls were not aggressive in their desire to score, she felt it was incumbent on her to go and get some points.

At times it seemed we were living in a circle, though. On the occasions when others would be on the cusp of stepping up, Shatara found it difficult to defer and allow them to spread their wings. She would be critical of their mistakes and they would retreat back inside their shells until they felt ready to try again.

To be successful as a team we were going to have to bridge the gap between a high-performing athlete and a cast of supporting players.

We made plenty of mistakes in the process, but we also learned how to more effectively manage the girls as they continued to grow. The girls also learned what they needed to do as well. Bridging our particular gap meant we were going to have to deal with two distinct areas: first, with the power of our star, and second, with our supporting cast.

How do you deal with your star and all of the other elements it takes to enjoy success? Here is what we discovered along the way.

Multiply success with multipliers. Stars like success. They define it by what they accomplish, and by the success of the broader group.

In business it is sales growth, manufacturing innovation and money. In basketball, wins and losses are the measuring stick used. Shatara needed to realize there was greater opportunity for her if the team around her had more success.

In our games, it did not take other teams long to figure out that if they shut Shatara down they would win the game. She would get her points, but they would not be enough to win.

To get Shatara involved in multiplying our success, we took time to point out to her that our team success increased when we had multiple players contributing.

She had to grasp that getting just fifteen points from our other perimeter players and ten from inside would put us in position to win plenty of games. We also had to emphasize that she would still get her twenty points, but it would come much more easily if the other team had to focus on players other than just her.

Highlight the detail people. There is more to basketball than just scoring points.

If you don't have defensive help, you will lose. It takes two people to break a press, even if one is just throwing the ball in. One girl can be blocked out from a rebound by a group, but it gets harder to keep three others from getting the ball.

No matter how much the stars might be delivering, they have to open their eyes and see that a team is behind their efforts, and without everyone else they won't shine quite as brightly, much less reach the bigger goals shared by everyone.

In business, your star may be the innovator, but without manufacturing and logistics support, his or her good ideas will stay on the shelf. Your top performer might be in sales and driving volume you only dreamed of, but to get the order completed, it takes a group of customer service people, accounts receivable staff to make sure you get paid, and don't forget the contributions purchasing and accounts payable make to keeping the ship sailing.

Stars, and those who manage them, need to grasp that success is not theirs alone, but a collective result that does not occur in a vacuum.

All-star teams are beatable. Imagine what your own collection of all-stars might look like. A seamless group with skills that defy description. Opportunities for success coming in so often you have to pick which ones to pursue. A faculty that will inspire students to win Nobel prizes. Ahhh...how sweet it would be. But how rare it is—not to put together teams loaded with only the best possible talent, but for results to meet expectations.

It is not that expectations are too high, but it is unrealistic in part to think a team of nothing but stars will be able to work cohesively as a unit. Think of how rare it is for the team with the most "talent" to win a championship in one of our major sports. The New England Patriots of 2007–08 were considered by many to be the finest football team of all time, until their run at perfection was derailed by the upstart New York Giants in the Super Bowl.

Most of you probably don't remember the 1976–77 Portland Trailblazers winning an NBA title against a "Who's Who" roster of the Philadelphia 76ers, a team that won their own title only after they downsized the superstar head count and found a few role players to make the team click.

The ultimate team victory of all time? The 1980 United States hockey team that won a gold medal in the Olympics and defeated what was considered the best collection of hockey talent ever in their foes from the USSR.

All these underdogs won because they understood team first and had leadership, both from coaches and players, which would not accept anything less than the ideal.

The brightest stars know they need help from others. The best managers of stars demand integration into the broader team. Why? To get the best outcome for everyone.

Let there be light. It is a crystal clear night and you are standing on your front porch when you see a light pass quickly through your line of sight. It is here and gone. Another star has just burned out and lost the luster it had. This is nature. It happens. It is not a bad thing unless it happens before it should.

Teams need stars. They are vital in so many ways to reaching your objectives.

If you have a star that keeps trying to shine but is held back too often, you will risk him or her either leaving your group or having his or her spirit broken.

In dealing with your stars, make sure you let them be who they are. Allow them to be creative and take chances. Seek their input on what more they can do to help raise the standards of the group.

While it takes the work of everyone to create success, the stars are going to be one of the key drivers in getting there, and if they don't have the respect they deserve from not only you, but those they interact with, then you have the potential for a real problem on your hands.

You have a goal to reach. This goal will be good for everyone involved. The reward might be financial or higher in purpose, but as you make decisions, make the best ones for all your players.

This means that sometimes there has to be a brighter light shining. Let your star carry the load he or she can, while you also challenge others to see what your bright light contributes. Point out the effort they put into what they do and the price they have paid for success.

If you can help others connect the dots between consistent effort, strong drive and innate skills, you may wind up having even more stars to manage than you ever realized.

Shatara is a gifted athlete and, more important, an outstanding young lady. She is going to be fun to watch through college and beyond because she will set high marks and work to reach them.

What has been most exciting to watch with Shatara, though, has been her ability to learn what it means to be one of several on a team and to trust in others to get things done while continuing to push herself to even higher levels of performance. Besides talent, she displays wisdom at a very young age.

Can you learn as well as Shatara?

I am enough of an artist to draw freely upon my imagination.
Imagination is more important than knowledge. Knowledge
is limited. Imagination encircles the world.
Albert Einstein

My philosophy is anyone or anything that
gives you knowledge inspires you.
Gabrielle Reece

It is impossible for a man to learn what he thinks he already knows.
Epictetus

The best way to have a good idea is to have lots of ideas.
Linus Pauling

Many ideas grow better when transplanted into another
mind than in the one where they sprung up.
Oliver Wendell Holmes

Receive my instruction, and not silver, And
knowledge rather than choice gold
Proverbs 8:10

Lesson Six: Good Ideas Can Come From Anywhere

"Time-out." We were in a close game and starting to look a little ratty, so it was time to take a break, get reorganized to stop the momentum of the other team, and make a few defensive adjustments.

The game was being played in a gym where there was little separation between the team benches and the seats our families had chosen for the night. In this setting, the parents had the unique opportunity to hear what we discussed with the girls and get a real feel for how things ebbed and flowed during play.

As is typical in our time-outs, we broke into two huddles, with Walker providing direction to the post players while I gave guidance to the perimeter positions. We then quickly came together to summarize it all before heading back on the floor.

We have a water girl who distributes bottles to the team during dead balls and takes care of their needs when they are not on the floor during play. Bethany is my youngest daughter and her older sister's junior by five years. She has spent quite a bit of time in gyms since her birth. She was hauled around to watch Meredith play basketball and volleyball before she could even roll over on her own.

She is also a good player locally in her own age group in both sports and has good instincts for any game she plays. She adores the Lady Titans and proudly assumes her duties as water girl every summer.

Bethany also takes advantage of our small roster size by scrimmaging with us most practices. In her mind there is no greater life accomplishment to be attained than being one of the girls on our team. The girls don't get this, but this is the way younger kids look at those just a few years older.

I share this with you to tell you how our time-out finished on this night.

We were wrapping our discussion up and about to send the girls back on the court when Bethany came walking through our huddle, collecting water bottles from the girls. As she passed through *very slowly*, her eyes were looking straight up at the ceiling. Talking to no one in particular, but loud enough for the parents, girls, Walker, and me to hear, she said, "Number 34 is scoring all their points in the laaaane...a zone might be better."

Behind the bench the parents laughed, and on the bench there was surprise she was paying such close attention to the game. Quickly realizing she was spot on, we revised the brilliant direction just given to be more in line with Bethany's observation.

It would have been easy to dismiss the thoughts of an elementary student and water girl, but she had the best idea and it was in our best interest to use it.

Many times and in many places, many people think that all good ideas start with them or within some hierarchy, and that there is no other source than them for good ideas.

In truth, great ideas can come from anywhere, and wise people are smart enough to snap them up when they are presented.

The challenge most of us face is getting these good ideas on our own while also encouraging the people around us to develop and express their thoughts. It is doable, but it is also a discipline and art that has to be practiced. Here are some thoughts to help you jump-start your creative process.

Identify the process you use. Think about the good ideas you have had. How many came from out of nowhere? Probably not many. So how did they develop?

Like most accomplishments in life, good ideas do not just drop out of thin air, but are the result of long thought, prior learning and a willingness to look at challenges in unconventional ways. Typically they come from a process that is practiced collectively or individually and, once conceived, can be vetted in the same ways.

Our plans for the Lady Titans are the result of a process. It is not structured, but there is an undeniable process to it.

It starts with Walker and me watching the girls' games during the school year as dads and seeing what they are doing well and who has developed new skills in their game.

Watching develops into talking about ideas, which are then processed by each of us as we go about doing life. When we see each other, we validate ideas or reject them for one reason or another. After a few weeks of this we sit down and create the playbook and notes we will provide the team. There is nothing formal about this process, but it is the one that has developed in our working relationship.

We also have a process we follow during tournaments. We play a game the first night, see a little of our competition that weekend, look at how the girls are doing and talk about it in the car on the way to the hotel.

The next morning, it is a good bet that one of us will be the first one in the hotel lobby from our group (partly to avoid waking our wives by working in the room) and will have a notebook in hand scribbling plays or making notes. It will not be long after that when the other appears and a discussion begins of changes we might make for the balance of the weekend.

We reach conclusions, share them with the girls, listen for their input and get moving. It is not formally established, but it works for what we are doing, and a definite process has emerged.

Besides the Lady Titans, another interest of mine is running. When a particular issue arises at work, home, or church, a resolution is usually found while out logging my miles.

Over the years it has become a time where ideas are sparked and pros and cons evaluated quietly in my mind without the distractions of a telephone, knock at the door, or all the other disruptions we are faced with when at a desk.

It has become an intentional place used for the purpose of exploring ideas. It is a little more intentional than what we do with the Lady Titans, and it is an effective practice most of the time.

What is the process you have for creating ideas? To get more good ideas, you need to understand how your other ones have been developed.

Making a list of ideas you have implemented and evaluating their results can help you see trends that differentiate the good outcomes from the less-than-positive ones.

Was there a place you went to think, a particular person you engaged in conversation, or some other common factor you can identify as helping you become more creative? If you want to keep good ideas coming, then allow that situation to arise on a consistent basis, especially when you need your best thoughts.

If you see there is a process that has worked for you in the past, then help others develop great ideas by spending time with them to assist them in the discovery of situations that help them do their best thinking. Then give them the freedom to go and create the ideas that will benefit the goals your team is pursuing.

I had a boss who understood this principle. He knew how to get my best when he wanted my input on something significant or noticed I was struggling with a problem.

He would tell me to make sure I got my run in that day. It worked for both of our benefits more times than not. My guess is you will find the same success if you turn your people loose wherever it is that they are the most creative. Rare is the person who finds the office to be that place.

Past knowledge coupled with continuing education keeps you sharp. Experience is wonderful. It provides a prism for viewing events with maturity and confidence.

Education is vital. If you don't know anything about something, you are not going to be able very often to contribute much that has value. Education may come from a classroom or be more hands on, but it is essential.

Can you imagine what it would be like to decide one day you had no need for additional experience or knowledge? Wow! How much would you miss out on?

To keep ideas flowing all of your life, you need to be a continual learner, because the world around you is in a state of constant change. Great ideas come from what we have knowledge of. If we have no knowledge of something, it is really difficult to have meaningful insights to solve problems.

When a person has education that meets with experience and comes in contact with new information, the potential for ground-breaking work is unleashed in ways that multiply dramatically.

Make a commitment to being a lifelong learner. There are any number of ways to fulfill this goal, but some of the ways you can are:

seek out new experiences;
read from sources that differ from your worldview;
make efforts to meet people with different experiences than yours;.
take classes in subjects you do not understand.

What is good for you is also good for others. If you want people to provide good ideas to you, then find ways for them to have the experiences above.

Allow your accounting people to participate with your sales staff at a trade show. Allow your sales force to work the night shift in one of your facilities.

Why is it that we think reading programs are only good for elementary students? Launch book clubs at the office where people from different disciplines read the same business book and then share their perspective on it. Challenge people in your organization to read something collectively and then submit one idea each based on what they read. Make it worth their while by awarding a prize to the best idea…even if it is not used.

Your goal is to get them jump-started in their thinking for the benefit of the organization. Another benefit to the ideas above is that they will cause people to step away from their e-mail and text messages and actually start talking. However, if you can't get them to meet face to face, it might also work to do an online discussion. This will help you network colleagues in far-flung locations that cannot meet with a group that is in another location.

Think of the collective imagination you can unleash if your people with experience and those just starting out start talking and sharing ideas.

Pay your dues. It has happened to many of us. You are in a meeting when someone above you on the organizational chart begins discussing a new idea. You listen and it sounds really familiar to you. It is one you shared with the person just a few weeks earlier that was dismissed almost out of hand as not being practical.

You want to scream, but you decide to hold it in. *Your* idea is considered brilliant, but the person getting the pat on the back fails to mention where he stumbled on the thought.

Those with management responsibilities have the opportunity to hear people's ideas and determine if they live or die. Good leaders know to make sure the author of an idea gets the credit he deserves. It is just plain smart.

When you give credit, you will inspire others to bring ideas they have. When you give credit, people want to work with you. When you give credit, you show you know how to bring the best out of the people you work alongside.

When an idea does not pan out, it is also important to accept responsibility for it. Own it yourself. When you own the ideas that don't work, you will keep your people inspired to be creative. If you let them walk off the edge of the world all alone, it has a tendency to make them a little more cautious in what they present to you.

Ideas are everywhere around you. The key is to make sure you have your ears open so you can hear them come from any person at any time. Even if it is the water girl.

I find my life is a lot easier the lower I keep everyone's expectations.
Bill Watterson

The quality of expectations determines the quality of our action.
A. Godin

You can't base your life on other people's expectations.
Stevie Wonder

I've always got such high expectations for myself.
I'm aware of them, but I can't relax them.
Mary Decker Slaney

High expectations are the key to everything.
Sam Walton

For surely there is a hereafter, And your hope will not be cut off.
Proverbs 23:18

Lesson Seven: Define Expectations

It was Friday morning around 11:00 a.m. when we talked first. Jessica was on the phone telling me how much fun she was having with some friends at the lake and asked if it would be all right if she missed the tournament that weekend. I told her it was her decision and not one that anyone else could make.

When we hung up, it was agreed she would call back within an hour with her decision because we were leaving mid-afternoon and needed to know what to expect.

The next call was to Walker to discuss the dilemma for the weekend. We would only have Lauren, Starr, Meredith, Landy and one other player we had recruited earlier in the week after Adrienne and Shatara each sprained an ankle at practice.

We talked about not making the trip with only five players, but we knew the healthy girls would want to play. After a few quick conversations and approval from my wife Rochelle, we decided our daughter Bethany would serve a dual role as water girl and emergency player.

Jessica called less than an hour later with her decision to stay where she was.

Jessica was in her first summer with the Lady Titans and had never really been part of a team that emphasized all we did about unity and commitment. The girls were not happy she was absent. They were mad. It would be fair to say that Jessica was a hot topic of their conversations a good bit of the weekend. When Meredith became sick after our first game, the talk grew even more heated.

Despite all of the positives that happened over the weekend, there was one thing Walker and I both knew. We now had a cloud hanging over the team. Jessica also knew she was in the midst of a storm with her friends when everyone returned home and her phone calls were going unreturned.

Before our next practice, Walker and I would be meeting with Jessica and her dad. There would have to be discipline for letting the team down, and it was going to be suspension from one game for every one she missed. It was going to be painful, because we were playing in Fort Smith next, making it easy for family and friends to come see the girls play, but she was going to be out for the weekend.

You don't learn much about people when things are going well. It is when things are difficult and hard that the real quality of a person comes through. Jessica Mays proved to be a person of extremely high quality.

When we met, she apologized right away, and her dad, Tim, did too. It was not qualified or rationalized. It was an apology. Her only concern was how to make amends with her friends.

I did not know Tim well before that day, but I knew after our meeting that I wanted to know his family better. He showed incredible class and character and did not once seek to change

68

the discipline we put in place. He only wanted to make sure things were made right with the team and Jessica.

After our discussion we went into the gym for practice, and Jessica trailed behind me, awfully sad and very apprehensive.

The girls were still cool as we sat down in a circle where each girl was asked to tell everyone about a time they made a mistake. They all had one. Most of them volunteered more than one. They all remembered what they wanted most at that point: redemption and forgiveness. They talked about how bad they hurt and how painful it was to hurt people.

They quickly figured out we all had been right where Jessica was. They all cried. They all hugged. We told them what Jessica's punishment was going to be. They all cried some more. They asked us to reconsider. We did not.

At the start of the conversation, a rock was placed in the middle of the circle. It was a good sized one and in the middle of it were the words "mistake rock." After we talked, the girls were told they could take the rock and throw it at Jessica, but they had to understand that if they did, they would have to allow others to do the same to them when they made a mistake.

No one touched the rock. Instead the girls all gathered around Jessica and hugged her. They told her they loved her. They apologized for being angry. She apologized for letting them down. We had one of the best practices ever.

The next weekend we were about to play our sixth and final game. Jessica had been incredible all weekend. She helped Bethany with the water, took care of the girls' towels and warm-ups. She encouraged them as they came to the bench. She was an inspiration.

Three minutes or so into our last game Walker called Jessica to go in the game. Her face had an odd mix of surprise and joy on it. The other girls just beamed. Before the game we told them Jessica had missed five games the week before and since this was our sixth, she would play in it. They were thrilled. We did not tell Jess because we wanted to see how she responded... and it was awesome. She played really well, too.

Jessica had learned the lesson of team. She has been the best teammate a person could have since then and has emerged as a leader for the high school team the girls play on. After one particularly rough game, she knew what they needed. She had them all over to spend the night and to get them laughing and talking and smiling.

It worked. They played better after a night together just being friends. She knew just what they needed. She knew it on her own and she did not need to be told to get it done. She knew it because she knew how much it meant to be part of a team.

Over the next several weeks, Walker and I spent much time discussing the "missed tournament" and how we got into that situation. As we talked there were critical lessons that emerged that need to be considered if you are working to create the best team possible or want to maximize your participation with a group. Here are a few of them.

Make sure people know what you expect. We give every family a list of expectations before we ever hold our first practice each year. It spelled out what was expected of the girls, the parents and the coaches.

Somehow, in the original set for that summer, it was clearly spelled out that the girls were expected to be at all practices unless they had a very good reason, but we made no mention of games. Who knows why? We just assumed they all knew how important it was to be at games, but we had not told them that.

When you are working with people and want to get the very best from them, it is critical that you make sure they not only know your key expectations, but also understand why they matter. If, when Jessica called, I had told her she was expected to be at the games, she would have been there. By not being clear with her, it became easy for her to assume it was not a problem if she was missing a particular weekend.

While some expectations may not have to be written down in our culture (tell the truth, don't steal...), the ones that might be fuzzy but are vital should be communicated clearly and consistently. If you are able to put in words the reason you have your expectation, the more likely people will work to make them happen.

If you are thinking about becoming part of something new and want a successful transition for everyone involved, then spend time understanding as fully as you possibly can what the expectations will be. Ask questions; learn why others have failed in the same situation you are considering. See if you can talk to people in the group beyond your primary contacts to gain their perspective on expectations.

By doing this prior to making a commitment, you are greatly improving the odds of success for you and those you are considering aligning with.

When you miss the mark, don't make excuses. Making an apology is one of the hardest things in the world to do.

The words "I'm sorry" are spoken, but right behind them comes the reason you did not get something right. You have heard it before, and probably said it yourself: "I'm sorry, but _____," or "I'm sorry. I _____." The blanks are filled in with a reason(s) why someone did not live up to expectations. In other words, "I'm sorry, but it is not my fault."

If you are saying "I'm sorry," then it is your fault. You might not have been able to control everything that happened, but stop with those first two words. The next words out of your mouth should be, "How can I make this right?" By the way, sometimes you won't be able to.

What Jessica did demonstrated just how tremendous a young lady she is. She owned the situation and actively went about making it right. That is a special gift.

Be ready to let it go. Have you ever made a mistake before? What response did you want from the people you let down? Were you hoping to be disparaged, chewed on, ignored? You probably wanted just a little grace. You probably wanted to find a hole to crawl into.

Why is it that we want this so badly when we make a mistake, but when others fail we want their head on a platter?

Maybe a better way to deal with people who don't meet your expectations is to give a little slack and teach them better for the future. If people are not delivering what you want from them, it may be that they are not the problem, but you are.

By not making sure they clearly understood what you wanted, you created an opportunity for them to fail. Teach better for the future and move on. Don't hang on to anger or resentment. They have no value for you or the person you are dealing with.

Understand there are consequences. It might be that you are the person who has done wrong. You have apologized appropriately and actively set about making things right. There may still be consequences to your actions that have to be accepted. It does not mean you are not forgiven by the people who were hurt. It just means you have to struggle through those consequences.

You may be the person who is moving on from a situation where your expectations were not met. You may still have to allow the person to suffer the consequences of what they did. You may want to let them off the hook, but you also have to maintain standards for the ultimate good of the larger group.

It is the acceptance of consequences that is becoming increasingly difficult for people to deal with. They want a no-fault method of living.

There have been several young ladies who have played with the Lady Titans, but the ones you have met are the core group. They are the ones who have been a part of the team consistently and passionately. They have bought in.

One young lady who was on the team our first year had real potential to be a great basketball player. She was athletic, tall and smart. During one game we called a time-out to talk about rebounding. We were being outhustled and just not getting the job done.

This girl was one of five not getting it done, but when they went back on the floor she was the only one not putting any additional effort into her rebounding.

After a minute or so, we took her out. When she got to the bench, I asked her about it and she snapped back, "I am rebounding." She spent the rest of the game on the bench pouting.

She had not met expectations, and her reaction was not appropriate for the situation. She did not get it.

This same girl approached me later to say she would miss our next five practices and the next three tournaments, but she would be with us for our final one, a trip to Colorado that was going to include some fun as a reward for a summer of hard work.

She was vague with her reason, and after talking it over with my assistant coach that year, we decided she really did not belong on the team. We told her she needed to turn everything in, and her reaction was indignant to say the least. The response of her father was also wrong. He wanted to know who we were to ask his daughter to turn in her stuff. Who were we to make these kinds of decision?

He had no issues with his daughter not meeting the expectations, but he did have issues with the consequences that came with his daughter's behavior. Compare this reaction to the humble and contrite one Jessica displayed. Which girl do you think will have the better outcome in life?

There are consequences to our actions. If people can learn from them, they will become better. They will also become more responsible.

There is a tomorrow. Five long games. Jessica had her uniform on but knew she had no chance of going in. She smiled and cheered her teammates on. She hustled water bottles. She did everything the girls did, but play. It had to seem like an eternity to her. When Jessica heard Walker call her name to go into the game, her heart was leaping inside.

Jessica had endured her consequences and was now back in the game. She was thrilled, her teammates were thrilled, and there were probably no two people more excited than Walker and I.

Why? Jessica showed she was a team player who would do whatever she could for the good of the team. She had overcome our inability to make the team's expectations clear. She showed us just how great a young lady she is.

It was a tough decision to share this story with you. It was tough because it might leave you with an impression of Jessica that is not right. Jessica and her family are to be admired because they have mastered the art in life of making things right when they go wrong. Have you mastered it yet, or are you still carrying a rock around looking for someone to throw it at? Be careful, because once you toss it, it can be thrown right back at you.

The best kind of friend is the kind you can sit on a porch
swing with, never say a word, then walk away feeling
like it was the best conversation that you ever had.
Unknown

Just because everything is different doesn't
mean anything has changed.
Irene Peter

Time, which changes people, does not alter
the image we have retained of them.
Marcel Proust

If nothing ever changed, there'd be no butterflies.
Author Unknown

Every beginning is a consequence—every
beginning ends something.
Paul Valery

And whoever compels you to go one mile, go with him two.
Matthew 5:41

Moving On

Starr was at the house last Saturday afternoon working on a school project with Meredith. Shatara joined in about 5:30 for dinner, and then they wanted to go see a movie. Sunday it was Meredith and Adrienne spending the afternoon together at her home. Jess was hanging out with her boyfriend of a year and Lauren was probably at the ball field watching the school's baseball team play in a tournament. Landy is a year behind the rest of them in school and hangs with a different crowd, but I bet she was having a great time with her friends. Bethany is now taller than Meredith, Starr and Landy while quickly catching the rest of the crowd.

Things have changed quite a bit for the Lady Titans since we started our journey together. Starr brought her jeep to the house and the girls went mudding in between homework and dinner. Shatara drove herself to the house, and when they went to the movie they didn't need someone to take them. When we first started, they had to ride bicycles to go anywhere without their parents. Boyfriends I have never gotten used to, and I still watch all of them with a suspicious eye, but for the most part the girls have made good choices in who they date.

One I did not care for even had the courage to come visit and talk about how he had changed. He had changed for the better, and Lauren was instrumental in it. The girls don't hang out with each other constantly because they have such varied interests, but they will always be there for each other. They are friends.

At least I think so. I also believe they know to watch each other's back and give respect as expected between people with common bonds. It is also my belief that they know trust is earned, and whatever path they take in life, they all have something to contribute wherever they may be. They also know to never quit and always, always keep fighting for each other. I think they know those things.

The hard part is discovering if they really do. There is only one way to know for sure if they get it or not: walk away and trust them to do what they know is right. Knowing when it is time to make the decision to walk away from our little gang is difficult, but as they mature into the outstanding young ladies they are, it becomes clear that now is the time. It is time because although they are mobile, they are still close enough to get help when they need it. It is time because they have shown themselves to be faithful to each other and their ideals when put to the test. It is time because there is just about no time left to admire how far they have come. It is time because there is always a time to walk away.

Learning life's lessons is a process. Practicing them is a challenge. It does not happen with just one talk at practice or several notes written to them, but has its genesis with great parents who teach it, a school that reinforces it and friends who believe it as much as you do. It takes effort, time and commitment to get it.

The girls show all the signs of getting it.

This is where the Lady Titans are now. It is time for Walker and me to walk away. To let them figure out "team" with each other as they prepare to leave home and make it on their own. By leaving them on their own, they become more responsible for their individual growth on the basketball court. It will also mean less of an opportunity for them to teach us all they do through their actions and the spirit that says they get it.

They get what it takes to be special.

Bethany and her group will now be the focus for Walker and me. I hope he stays for as long as the trip is fun for him.

It will be different.

This next group has more skill at their age than the Lady Titans did. They have more trophies and awards. There are more of them. But will they be fortunate enough to have what made Lauren, Starr, Meredith, Adrienne, Shatara, Jessica, and Landy so uniquely special? Hearts as big as you will ever find. Commitment to each other. A never-say-die attitude. Last of all, the ability to teach so much simply through their character.

I hope so—and if they do, it will be a real privilege to be along for the ride.

www.ingramcontent.com/pod-product-compliance
Lightning Source LLC
Chambersburg PA
CBHW071248170526
45165CB00003B/1284